Brimming with creative inspiration, how-to projects, and useful information to enrich your everyday life, Quarto Knows is a favorite destination for those pursuing their interests and passions. Visit our site and dig deeper with our books into your area of interest: Quarto Creates, Quarto Cooks, Quarto Homes, Quarto Lives, Quarto Drives, Quarto Explores, Quarto Gifts, or Quarto Kids.

© 2020 Quarto Publishing Group USA Inc.

Produced in 2020 by becker&mayer!, an imprint of The Quarto Group,
11120 NE 33rd Place, Suite 201, Bellevue, WA 98004 USA.
www.QuartoKnows.com

becker&mayer! kids titles are also available at discount for retail, wholesale, promotional, and bulk purchase. For details, contact the Special Sales Manager by email at specialsales@quarto.com or by mail at The Quarto Group, Attn: Special Sales Manager, 100 Cummings Center Suite 265D, Beverly, MA 01915 USA.

20 21 22 23 24   5 4 3 2 1

ISBN: 978-0-7603-6893-0

Library of Congress Cataloging-in-Publication
Data is available.

Author: L.J. Tracosas
Illustrator: Turine Tran

Printed, manufactured, and assembled in Shenzhen, China, 10/20
338461

ESCAPE THIS BOOK

The Cursed Castle

Search the pages for clues that will help you find the occupants of the castle and reverse the curse! Solve the room puzzles one by one to discover the correct path through the castle. Be on the lookout for clues as you go. Solving the room puzzles in the correct order will help you piece together the clues you need to save the kingdom!

Ahead of you lies the castle. Yesterday, you received a scroll, delivered by a hooded squire.

There's a curse upon the castle that only you can lift. Until then, the halls of the castle, even the throne, lie empty—save for the clues you need to break the curse.

It was written in a strange hand, signed only with the royal seal. When you looked up from the scroll, the squire had vanished.

You rode as fast as you could to the royal city. Now, it lies ahead of you. Everything depends on you.

Your mind flashes to the royal court and courtiers, the smithy and the knights, the guards and kitchen staff, the citizens. Your friends, your family.

Armed with nothing but your mind and a map of the castle, you begin.

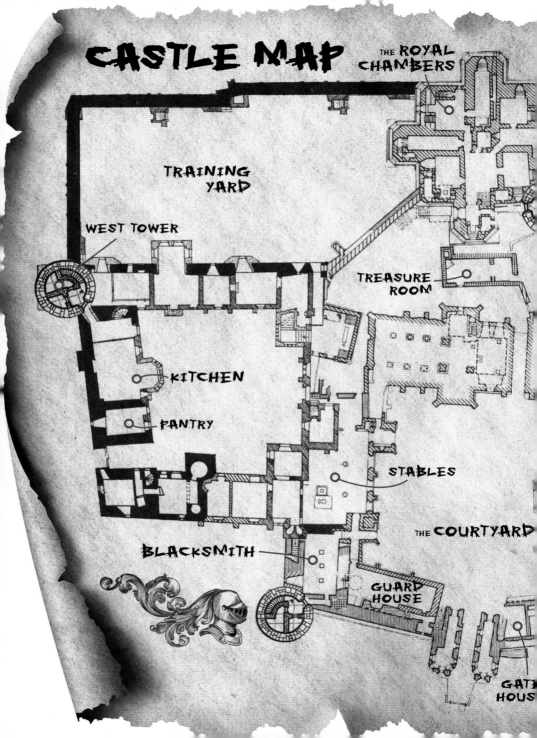

CASTLE MAP

THE ROYAL CHAMBERS

TRAINING YARD

WEST TOWER

TREASURE ROOM

KITCHEN

PANTRY

STABLES

THE COURTYARD

BLACKSMITH

GUARD HOUSE

GATE HOUSE

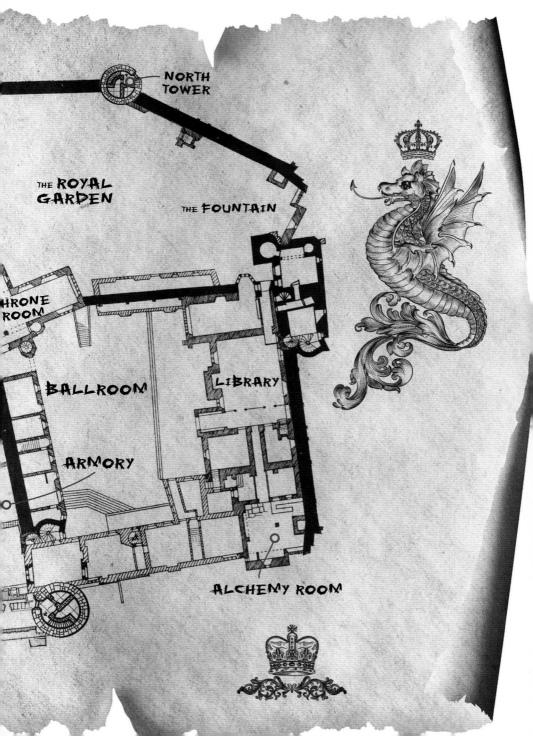

NORTH
TOWER

THE **ROYAL
GARDEN**

THE **FOUNTAIN**

THRONE
ROOM

BALLROOM

LIBRARY

ARMORY

ALCHEMY ROOM

LOCATIONS

The courtyard is eerily silent. A slight breeze blows, rustling the grass, trees, and abandoned hay. This courtyard holds a clue—you can feel it—but spotting it is going to be like finding a needle in a haystack.

Training Yard

THE COURTYARD

North Tower

West Tower

9

Ballroom

Blacksmith

15

Armory

GATE HOUSE

You enter this castle
Like you enter a book
Turn to the cover
And take a close look

Get ready! Look high!
What towers above you?
By windows, not doors,
You'll find your next clue.

Guard House

11

The pantry no doubt once burst with abundance. Your stomach growls thinking about food. As you look around, you imagine what this place might have looked like. When you read the sign, you have an idea.

Garden

Fountain

PANTRY

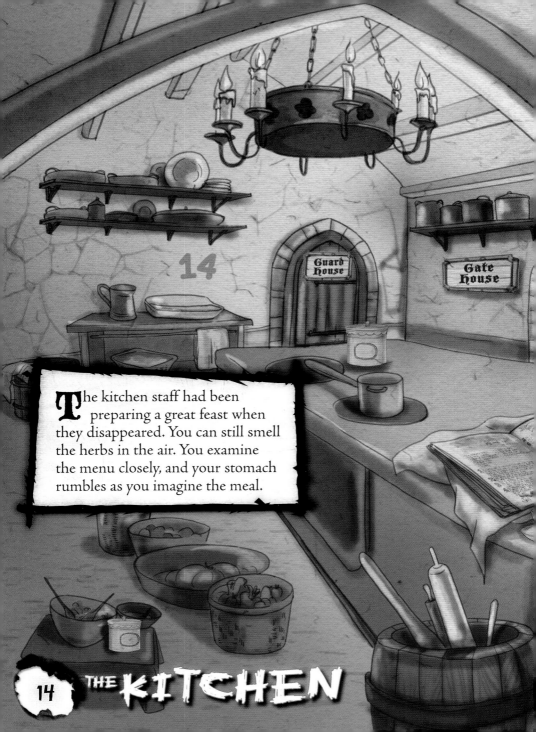

The kitchen staff had been preparing a great feast when they disappeared. You can still smell the herbs in the air. You examine the menu closely, and your stomach rumbles as you imagine the meal.

14

Guard House

Gate House

14 THE KITCHEN

Hamhock with greens & quail egg
Orange-glazed steak of caribou
Upside down frittata
Seared fowl with cauliflower
Emplumeus & Custard

Pantry

15

The smell of old books surrounds you in the library. The wisest people in the kingdom have studied here. For a moment, you wish one of them could be here now to help you solve this mystery. But you take a deep breath. You can do this. You can find the answer.

BEANS
BREAD
BREAKFAST
BUTTER
CARROT
CHERRY
CHICKEN
DINNER
EGGS
FISH
LETTUCE

LUNCH
MEAT
PEAR
PIE
POTAT
STEW
TOMA

16 LIBRARY

rmory

A B C D E F G h i J K L M N O P Q R S T U V W X Y Z

B	A	O	S	R	Y	L	R	C	E
H	R	G	T	R	E	E	E	C	B
N	G	E	R	A	T	N	U	H	R
E	W	E	A	T	T	T	N	S	E
K	H	E	U	K	T	O	M	I	A
C	Y	B	T	E	F	A	P	F	D
I	R	O	L	S	N	A	E	B	O
H	C	A	R	R	O	T	S	M	E
T	O	M	A	T	O	M	T	I
C	N	U	L	S	R	A	E	P

As you enter the blacksmith's workroom, you shiver. The smithy's fires have gone out for the first time since the castle was built. Suddenly, you notice a message etched in iron.

Stables

BLACKSMITH

Treasury

Training
Yard

Royal
Chambers

9

LOOK TO THE
SPINE THAT HAS
NO BONES

19

The throne sits empty for the first time in history. Without the ruler commanding attention, you notice symbols on the throne. You know you've seen them before. But where? You might need to retrace your steps. Then you can move on.

THRONE ROOM

Pantry

Alchemy

22 GUARD HOUSE

You hurry through the guard house, wondering if the castle's curse is still alive. Your home village was safe when you left. The best way to protect them, you decide, is to save the castle. You wonder if a direct attack is the best way.

West Tower

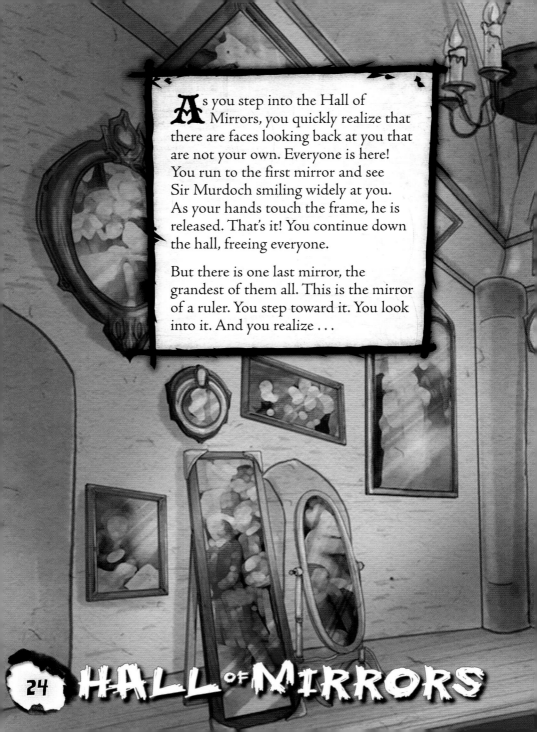

As you step into the Hall of Mirrors, you quickly realize that there are faces looking back at you that are not your own. Everyone is here! You run to the first mirror and see Sir Murdoch smiling widely at you. As your hands touch the frame, he is released. That's it! You continue down the hall, freeing everyone.

But there is one last mirror, the grandest of them all. This is the mirror of a ruler. You step toward it. You look into it. And you realize . . .

HALL OF MIRRORS

You played in this garden as a child, running between the hedges with your friends. You know what to do.

Stables

THE GARDEN

Gate House

Kitchen

27

You climb the West Tower, hoping for a better view. Sometimes, looking at a problem from a different angle can shed new light on it. Your footsteps on the stairs echo against the walls. You survey the courtyard. Then a thought dawns on you.

Stables

WEST TOWER

The riches of the kingdom twinkle in the torchlight in front of you. Even though some gems spill onto the floor, you can't help but think about how organized it all is. Almost like there is a pattern. If you can figure it out, maybe you'll see what is missing. Maybe you'll find another clue.

West Tower

Garden

22

TREASURY

30

Royal Chambers

Library

Kitchen

North Tower

Guard House

31

TRAINING YARD

You smile as you step into the Training Yard. You've always had an archer's eye. You could be happy spending hours here, just nocking your arrows and firing your bow, hitting bull's-eye after bull's-eye. But now you need to focus on the next target.

Garden

34 ARMORY

The suits of armor wait for their owners, each piece of iron and chainmail molded especially for the knight who wore it. Even now, the well-polished pieces glint and gleam like the royal treasure. You see the Roman army on the wall and wonder if their success would translate to your own.

13

ROYAL CHAMBERS

The royal chambers are a most peaceful place. They were built to be a place where a ruler could retire from the bustle of castle life, and meditate on what matters most to the kingdom. As you gaze upon your surroundings, you know that you too must think about what matters most here. Maybe that will help you move on.

Throne Room

Fountain

Garden

Blacksmith

Treasury

ALCHEMY ROOM

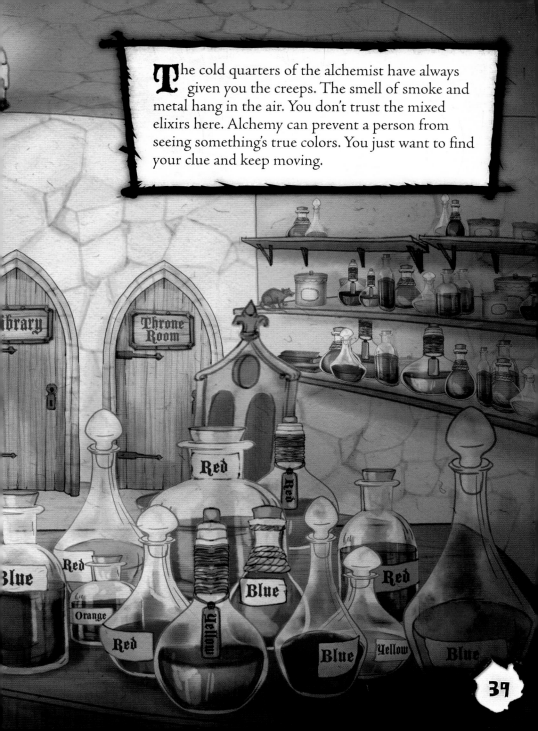

The cold quarters of the alchemist have always given you the creeps. The smell of smoke and metal hang in the air. You don't trust the mixed elixirs here. Alchemy can prevent a person from seeing something's true colors. You just want to find your clue and keep moving.

THE STABLES

Garden

Throne Room

In the stables, even the horses are gone. Saddles are abandoned in the stalls. You pound your fist on the stable doors in anger. Whoever is playing this cursed game doesn't know who they're up against. The next move is yours.

"Hello?" you call, even though you know the only answer you'll get is your echo. Music and merriment once filled these halls. Now all you find is silence. You want to hurry from the ballroom and its cold emptiness, but there are so many ways to go. You study two portraits of the duchess. Will your quest make a difference to her?

Courtyard
1

Alchemy
2

Treasury
3

West Tower
4

THE BALLROOM

5
North
Tower

22

Library

8

Kitchen

6

Pantry

7

43

You find yourself at the fountain—a perfect spot to collect your clues and reflect on all you've learned. Your mind races, ideas rain down. You are so close to breaking the curse, you can feel it.

THE FOUNTAIN

45

PUZZLE GLOSSARY

There are hundreds of types of puzzles in the world! Here are some examples. Can you find them in this book?

Logic Puzzles: In a logic puzzle, you must follow a series of provided rules to reach a unique and specific solution.

Grid Puzzles: In this type of puzzle, a partially completed grid provides guidelines, or rules, to the puzzler. An example is Sudoku, in which a 9 x 9 square consisting of nine 3 x 3 squares must be filled in by the numbers 1-9 without repeating a number vertically, horizontally, or within each 3 x 3 square.

Syllogisms: A syllogism uses a series of statements assumed to be true to allow you to arrive at a conclusion using logic. An example would be: "All men are mortal. John is a man. Therefore…"

Pattern Puzzles: Similar to logic puzzles, pattern puzzles require you to identify the pattern in a series of items. You may be asked to figure out the missing symbol in the pattern.

Odd One Out: Odd one out puzzles are a type of pattern puzzle in which you must spot the item or symbol that does not fit the pattern.

Therefore, John is a mortal.

Riddles: A riddle is a question or statement that has a hidden meaning. Examples include:

1. What comes down but never goes up?

2. What word is spelled incorrectly in every dictionary?

Seek and Find Puzzles: Seek and find puzzles include word searches, spot-the-difference comparisons, and other visual puzzles.

Word Puzzles: Word puzzles use elements of language, such as words and letters. Hangman is one example.

Acrostic: In an acrostic, the first or last letter or syllable of each word or line spells out a message.

Anagrams: Word puzzles where you rearrange an assortment of letters. For example, if you rearrange the letters in "listen," you can create the word "silent."

Ciphers: Ciphers are word puzzles where you replace a letter with another letter or symbol according to a certain rule. For example: A=1, B=2, C=3, etc. Or A=Z, B=Y, C=X, etc. Any rule can be used, as long as you are consistent.

Other puzzles you may find in this book: chess, mazes, counting, and identifying the parts of a whole.

1. Rain
2. Incorrectly

ANSWERS

Oh no! You've stumbled into the lair of the dark wizard who cursed the castle! He has all the answers, but reading them might come at a terrible price . . .

Are you sure you want to read on? You can always stop by the pull tabs at the back of the book for hints or check the Puzzle Glossary on page 46 for fresh ideas to solve your puzzle.

If you're sure, read on!

The Courtyard is a seek-and-find puzzle and an anagram puzzle. Unscrambled, the letters in both haystacks tell you to go to . . .

The West Tower

The Gate House is a riddle. The answer takes you to the book's cover, where tiny letters in the towers direct you to . . .

The Ballroom

The Pantry is a counting puzzle. The sign on the wall says take 7. When you find an item there is 7 of, match it to a door with the corresponding symbol, which is the …

The Treasury

The Kitchen is an acrostic puzzle with two acrostics. Use the first and last letters of each line on the menu to spell out …

The Guard House

The Library is a word search. Once you have found all the words, the leftover letters tell you to go to …

The Alchemy Room

The Blacksmith is another riddle, which sends you to the spine of the book where you find "TY", sending you to …

The Training Yard

The Throne Room has symbols that are also in the Library. If you refer to the cipher on the book spines, you will translate the symbols to RC, which sends you to …

The Royal Chambers

The Guard House is an odd-one-out puzzle. There are offensive weapons by two doors and a defensive weapon by the correct door, which is …

The Pantry

The Garden is a maze. It leads to …

The Gate House

The West Tower's puzzle has hints in the text to send you to the illuminated door …

The Armory

The Treasury is a logic puzzle, like Sudoku. Instead of numbers, the grid uses different colored gems. Each one can only be used once in each row, column, and 3x3 segment. The gem that goes in the highlighted square will correspond to the gem on the correct door, which is …

The Library

The Training Yard is a pattern puzzle. The correct door is painted with the next piece of the pattern that begins on the targets, which is …

The Throne Room

The Armory is a tough one! The text sends you to the Roman Numerals. Translate the Roman Numerals to numbers, then to letters (1=A, 2=B, etc.), which sends you to …

The Stables

The Royal Chambers is a counting puzzle. The text hints that the "most" counted item is correct. The item with the most is the water pitchers, sending you to …

The Fountain

The Alchemy Room is another tough one! If you study the labels, you'll notice the liquids and the colors do not match. There is one bottle whose label is not contained in the standard primary colors. The name of the correct door matches the liquid in this bottle …

The Blacksmith

The Stables is a chess game. The horse chess piece moves a certain way in chess, which corresponds to an item placed in the stable: the rose, which sends you to …

The Garden

The Ballroom is a spot-the-differences puzzle. There are 6 differences in the portraits, which leads you to …

The Kitchen

The Fountain has no puzzle of its own. The blanks on the wall are a place for you to take the 17 clues you found in the previous 17 pages and solve what they mean in order to solve the book. The 17 clues are the green numbers. Each of them is a cipher, where the number equals a letter: 1=Z, 2=Y, etc. When those letters are put in the correct order, you get a message:

To solve, make it Rain

The Fountain, part 2: When you have solved the message, you can make the fountain rain by flipping the page over, where the number 24 is revealed. Go to that page to solve the book.

The Book: What do you see in a mirror?